A Child's Moon

California Poets in the Schools
San Joaquin Valley

Betsy Lee
Editor

Sponsored in part by a grant from

Lodi Arts
COMMISSION

Library of Congress Cataloging-in-Publication Data

A child's moon : California poets in the schools : San Joaquin Valley /
Betsy Lee, editor. Jewel of the valley : a California anthology / J.
Jackson Harvey, editor.
p. cm.
Added t.p. title: Jewel of the valley.
Works published back-to-back with separate title pages.
Added t.p. title: Jewel of the valley.
ISBN 0-9667532-4-0 (pbk.)
1. American poetry–California–San Joaquin Valley. 2. San Joaquin Valley
(Calif.)–Poetry. 3. California–Poetry. I. Title: Jewel of the valley. II. Lee, Betsy, 1957-
III. Harvey, J. Jackson. IV. Title: Jewel
of the valley.
PS571.C2 C47 2002
811'.608097455–dc21

2002009220

ISBN 0-9667532-4-0

BLUE MOON PRESS
LODI, CALIFORNIA
A SUBSIDIARY OF BLUE MOON - LEE PRESS
BLUMOONP@AOL.CO

FORWARD . . .

The name, *A Child's Moon,* is an English term for the moon when it appears in the daytime . . . when a child might be awake and able to see it.

The poetry in this book is a lot like a child's moon it that it is more than the study of classical poetry. This is the work of students who have had the opportunity to see poetry as a means of expressing their own ideas, dreams and emotions. It's the poetry of their own skies. The five or ten week classes presented poetry in the classroom but it also gave opportunity for students to write and to perform their own works of poetry.

This book is the collected works of students who have been a part of the classes of California Poets in the Schools. As a Poet in Residence from Lodi, California I have been teaching in a number of schools in the San Joaquin Valley with the funding of a generous grant from the Lodi Arts Commission. The students in different schools during the 2001-2002 school year submitted poetry and the presented poems are an anthology of selected works.

Like a child's moon, these poems are seen through the eyes of students and are just as important and beautiful as a full moon in an afternoon sky. And like a child's moon, this book held in the hands of the young poets will be something they will remember and treasure all their lives and so will we.

Betsy Lee
EDITOR

BLUE MOON PRESS WOULD LIKE TO GIVE CREDIT TO:

Allyson Rae Green . . . *Cover*

Allyson Rae Green "Ally" is a twelve year old who resides with her family in Central Florida. She attends Winter Springs Junior High School and enjoys art, music, and dance. Her artwork has been displayed in numerous exhibits as well as in competitions in Florida and Kentucky.

CALIFORNIA POETS IN THE SCHOOLS . . .

is the largest writers-in-the-schools program in the nation bringing approximately one hundred and fifty poet-teachers into California classrooms. Nearly 25,000 students each year are involved in CPITS programs.

In this anthology are the poems of students from a number of San Joaquin Valley schools. As you read the book you will note some themes repeated in the work of the students, this is because of the Poet-Teacher's choice of curriculum used in the workshop/classes.

These classes included the "I AM" poem which had a certain form to follow. The common themes in the poetry reflected the study of watersheds, environment and the night sky in Northern California, the response to works of art brought into the classroom and even the visit of an eight foot boa constrictor named Luna.

In addition to this book, some of the classrooms produced their own thirty-two page stapled chapbooks or had displays of their poetry in their school cafeterias or classrooms. One school held a poetry show with more than one hundred and fifty persons in attendance as students read their poems to family and friends.

CALIFORNIA POETS IN THE SCHOOLS ENDEAVORS TO:

· make creative writing and art an integral part of the educational lives of young people.

· encourage young people to value culture, perception, artistic integrity, and creativity; and express themselves freely.

· provide students with role models demonstrating the importance of creative writing and art.

· share and affirm the cultural diversity of California by hiring a diverse group of poets and artists, as well as by bringing multicultural materials into the classroom.

A CHILD'S MOON
TABLE OF CONTENTS

Leaves, Leaves

Merritt Huff
3rd Grade

Leaves, leaves
all around.

Falling, falling
to the ground.

Where do they come from?
I don't care.

I don't think they come from anywhere.

The Snake

Justine Chacon
6th Grade

The snake pushes.
It wiggles and shoves.
Its scaly skin
Just won't budge.

It tries to relax
Its tongue makes a flicker
It wishes its skin
Would shed off much quicker.

It decides to push
More than before
Finally, miraculously,
Its skin flops to the floor.

Daytime Moon

Spenser Schaffner
7th Grade

If you see a moon in the daytime,
It's a really funny sight.
If you see a moon in the daytime,
It would be a child's delight!

Alphabet Snake

Spenser Schaffner
7th Grade

My snake can make an "o"
My snake can make a "k"
My snake can make a "b"
And a really good "a"
My snake can make an "s"
My snake can do his "y"s
But however hard he tries,
He simply cannot dot his "i"s

Long Before Our Time

Betsy Lee

it is not by accident
that I am here today

I planned this
long before my birth

where you would hear
and I would recite
and poetry is what would be painted

poetry is consumed
ears feel
eyes hear
mouths listen
words are never by accident

I planned this long before my birth

La Loca Luna
The Crazy Cheese Moon
Betsy Lee

This silver ball in the sky
this orb
this distant bright mystery
this moon
is really made of cheese, you know?
A good mozzarella,
a swiss,
a cheddar
or maybe blue cheese . . .
(there is such a thing as a blue moon, ya know?)

I am sure, convinced,
absolutely entangled in thought.
My head is filled with hundreds of miles of wires
computer chips and floppy disks
connecting thought and fiction
and I know . . .
I know, Saturn is also a cheese ball on a cracker.

I once stood on the moon,
far away and distant.

When I returned to earth
I went to the store
bought all the cheese I could fit in my frig.

Now, I am older . . .
I just stand in the night,
looking up to the moon,
dreaming . . .
longing to go home.

when the world around me
doesn't always make sense
I will curl up on the old porch swing
the gentle rocking back and forth
takes me among tree branches
soon the smell of the old spruce tree returns
a light breeze on my face
it is never far away
I am a child again

Everything Will Be Okay

Laurie Wright
8th Grade

Rising before me,
close enough to touch,
the silver orb hangs low in the sky.
Shimmering softly it provides comfort.
Somehow it tells me that everything will be okay.
The crickets, chirping softly, provide reassurance,
telling me that life will go on.
As water drips from my eyes,
wetting my cheeks,
I think about life.
How people change, and
everyday things you thought you could count on
suddenly disappear.
The tears come faster, I can taste the salt.
Sobs rise unchecked in my throat,
racking throughout my body.
I cry for the best friends,
who are lost to you forever.
I cry because life hurts.
As the crickets continue to chirp softly,
my tears cease to fall.
Life will go on, they chirp.
And as I gaze up to that silvery orb,
hanging low in the sky,
close enough to touch,
it tells me that everything will be okay.
Everything will be okay.

The Leaves

Lilian Wing Liu
4th Grade

The wind carries the leaves through the air
like a fast plane going across my head,
red leaves,
orange,
yellow,
green,
many,
many colorful shapes,
sizes,
sounds,
and colors.
The leaves falling down from trees
are like . . .
raindrops falling from the clouds.
Soon all the leaves turn into another color:
brown.
The leaves turn crispy and crunchy,
I rake them up,
and jump into the pile.

The Moon

Sarah Ponte
7th Grade

The moon is big,
The moon is round,
The moon is yellow,
Sometimes orange,
The moon is the world's night-light,
One big light,
with the background of one starry night.

Raindrop

Sarah Ponte
7th Grade

As I fall from the sky,
I am separated from my family,
We gently coat the earth,
And just as we settle,
We disappear like magic,
Deep into the earth's soil.

I Am Captain Scott O'Grady

Scott Griffith
8th Grade

I am Captain Scott O'Grady.
I wonder would I survive?
I hear the gun shots.
I see blood around me.
I want to get away.
I am Captain Scott O'Grady.

I pretend to be the ground.
I feel hunger strike.
I worry about my family.
I cry silent tears.
I am Captain Scott O'Grady.

I understand why I am not rescued.
I say, "God please help me!"
I try to call out to the heavens.
I hope I can go home.
I am Captain Scott O'Grady.

The Night Sky

Jacob Lane
3rd Grade

Moon
very beautiful
The moon is very bright
clear night
stars

If I Were a Raindrop

Britney Erwin
8th Grade

If I was a raindrop
I would be a tear from the sky
falling from very high
saying good-bye
to my family and friends
but I tend
to mend
when I come to the end
and fall to the ground
and hear the loud sound
I still miss my family and friends
I am a raindrop!

Untitled

Khush Singh
8th Grade

Listen my child to the wind,
hear what it is saying,
it is saying to protect your mother,
your mother earth.

An enemy has come to destroy her,
it cuts her trees,
kills her animals,
and pollutes her air.

Her grass is no longer green,
her water
is no longer.
This enemy of hers is blind,
it does not know what it is doing.

So save her my child,
she is dying,
and one day she shall not be.

One

Kody Oppendike
8th Grade

I see the moon,
I see the sun,
are they two or are they one?

I'm the Night Sky

Korine Bobrow
3rd Grade

I'm the night sky
looking down on you.
When the sun comes up
I'm still watching.
I'm watching in the spring,
I'm watching in the winter.
Even when you're not looking,
I will sneak up behind you
and say BOO ! ! ! !
Some times I scare you,
Some times I don't,
I am the night sky
looking down on you . . .

I Am A Rain Drop

Imroz Sanahu
3rd Grade

I am a rain drop.
My rain drop friends
come with me in a cloud.
When the cloud gets too heavy,
we all fall down.
I fall in a river,
with my friends.
We rush down a river.
The river flows into a bay.
The bay flows into the Pacific Ocean.
We all are together.
The rainbow came up,
we all thought it was pretty.

Raindrop

Jordan Newman
4th Grade

If I were a raindrop
I would see the seas flowing
down from me.
I would hear
the waves roaring at me.
The thunder blinking at me.
And trees whistling at me.
I could hear the others dropping,
I am a raindrop.

Trees

Darla Roth
5th Grade

The leaves falling are like soft clouds that drift slowly.
The wind carries the leaves through the air
like feathers dancing down
at a pace so elegant and nice.
The leaves on a summer tree
look like branches full of wonder,
waiting to come down.
Trees are as big as animals so great and wise.
Trees sound like the soft wind,
whispering to you like a message in your mind.

Snake

Andrew Dunbar
6th Grade

Slithers in the forest
No legs
Agile
Killer bite
Extremely hungry

I am a Basketball

Curtis Yamanaka
4th Grade

I am a basketball.
I wonder about the game.
I hear bong bong.
I see the basketball court going up and down.
I want to get off this court to soothe my head.
I am a basketball.

I pretend I'm not here.
I feel like I have a headache.
I worry about when they won't choose me.
I cry mommy!
I am a basketball.

I understand players have to play basketball.
I say stop stop timeout.
I try to go flat.
I hope it will be 2.2 seconds in the 4th.
I am a basketball.

Raindrops

Cynric Cho
8th Grade

As I travel through the dense mist,
I feel one drop, two drops, and more.
Then I hear the thunder roar.
The thunder makes the storm seem like
a mother crying for her children.
But no matter
how much she cries,
the children will not stay.
Down, down, the droplets travel.
Into the ground, combining and becoming one.
Forming into creeks,
forming into rivers.
Crying out to the ocean,
"Wait for me! Wait for me!"
And so the raindrops travel now,
as many and as one,
into the open arms of the sea.
Glassy, sparkling, perfect.
The ocean, many and one.

Untitled

Cynric Cho
8th Grade

The milky white,
the brightness,
the sorrow and the calm.
The orb,
of milky fire,
brightens my way home.

I Am A Teacher

Lindsay Salazar
7th Grade

I am a teacher.
I wonder how kids have so much energy
at the end of the day.
I hear kids laughing, playing, and sometimes they're quiet.
I see beautiful bright little children.
I want the best for them.
I am a teacher.

I pretend I am their mother.
I feel strongly to be a good role model.
I worry they will turn out bad.
I cry for the fear of my worries coming true.
I am a teacher.

I understand my place in this world.
I say to myself, "They understand."
I try to make them feel happy.
I hope they will grow up to be the best they can possibly be.
I am a teacher.

The Moon Is Love

Jaime Gamez

The moon is a white ball.
It is an angel's wing.
It is a ball of cheese.
The moon is lovely.

Trees

Alyssa Musto
5th Grade

The leaves are like snow balls on my face,
they are very gentle.
The winds carries the leaves through the air
like birds flying gently and slow.
The leaves on a summer tree look like a
beautiful colorful rainbow.
Trees are big as giants,
tall and big.
Trees sound like a whistle
when the wind goes through them.
The sunlight through the trees
looks like a puzzle of a sunset all put together.

Baby

Alyssa Musto
5th Grade

Wet drops are coming from my eyes.
We walk until we see what we are looking for.
Now everybody has drops coming from their eyes.
The baby is gone.
He has left us.
Gone to heaven above.
Baby

Leaves

Nicole Truong
3rd Grade

The leaves
falling
are like a beautiful feather.

The wind
carries
the leaves through the air like birds flying.

The leaves
on a summer tree
look like a colorful rainbow.

Trees
are
as big as a two story house.

Trees
sound
like animals rustling in the bushes.

The sunlight
through the trees
looks like sunset.

Hector

Amelia Goodfellow
7th Grade

My snake is a vegetarian
With the name of Hector
He craves all day for one taste of
potatoes with chives and pepper.

He salivates for tomato juice
And drools for garlic mushrooms
He loves the taste of fresh green beans
And ere thy garden blooms.

So what if Hector's a little odd?
No appetite for rats
So what if he's a little weird?
He's nothing compared to my cat!

Metamorphosis

Amelia Goodfellow
7th Grade

Flowing
Cycling, Spirals, Swirling through the Air
Freedom lasts
Until the Bay
Joined in unity
Bonded molecules
Structured circles
Churning, minute
Drops are one, then
Evaporation
Resurrected as a birth
Power
Free again, at last, alone.

The Moon, The Sky, The Stars

Kristin Lieb
8th Grade

Laying on the grass,
the moon above me,
the sky around me.
I can feel everything,
see everything,
hear everything.
As I lay here on the grass,
the soft soil beneath me,
the whispering wind surrounding me.
I fade from my body,
drift to the sky,
the moon,
the stars.
I am everything,
this joyful feeling,
this lust,
this dream.
I understand the universe,
as we are now one.
Nothing is confusing me,
I feel no hate,
no pain.
This remembrance of feelings brings me back,
brings me to my body,
and as I am once again reunited as whole,
I only wish to be where I was before,
to be away from this world,
to feel only happiness, love.
But at least I know I can go there for a little while,
even if only to be away for a moment,
a fraction of a dream . . .

The Moon, The Night

Ngoc-Anh Le
8th Grade

Beaming on earth.
Giving light to the night,
making shadows on the ground.
Trees are still, night is quiet
as moon slowly rises,
the sun slowly sets.

I Am a Raindrop That Falls From the Sky

Daniel Jones
3rd Grade

I can be in the water.
I can be in you.
I am a rain drop.
I can be a color.
I can be in a bug.
I can be a snow flake.
I am a rain drop.

I am Jack

Kirk Sasaki
3rd Grade

I am Jack.
I wonder if Kirk is really my friend?
I hear a basketball.
I see a dog.
I want pizza for dinner.
I am Jack.

I pretend to be a drummer.
I feel very lucky.
I worry about my dog.
I cry gold out of my eyes.
I am Jack.

I understand everything.
I say, "Da dan ta da."
I try to stay alive.
I hope to win a basketball game.
I am Jack.

Rain

David Contreras
6th Grade

Remarkable
Awesome
Invincible
Neat

Stillness at Night

Jennifer Sudweeks
8th Grade

I am standing underneath a giant oak tree.
Grabbing the cool, rough bark, I hoist myself up.
The few leaves that linger rustle slightly.
I find a seat and peer through the branches
reaching for the sky.

The great moon is looming above me.
Its pale light casts shadows everywhere.
Through the dimness of it all,
I can see a small rabbit scurrying through the shrubs.

An owl hoots above me, and circles the sky.
He flaps silently through the stillness of the night.
Then, sighting his prey, he dives.
Devouring the small animal, he hoots with delight.

A few minutes pass, then an hour, then two.
With a sigh I glance at my glowing watch.
I slip out of the branches, ready to go home,
And to leave my peaceful spot.

I trudge through the tall grass,
Crunching the crisp leaves underfoot.
I hate to leave this place, but don't worry
Tomorrow when the moon is high, I will return.

Nighttime

Stephanie J. Maynard
7th Grade

It is nighttime
My time
A time to think about my inner self
A time to ponder who I am
A time to listen to my thoughts
A time to dream

I Am Alone

Stephanie J. Maynard
7th Grade

I am alone
I wonder if any one cares
I hear friends laughing, playing together
I see my life rushing past me
I want to be understood and welcomed
I am alone

I pretend I am someone else
I feel alone in this place called Earth
I worry that my life, as I know it will end
I cry that I am different, and the world has shut me out
I am alone

I understand that I am only one to face the world alone
I say everything is OK
I try to become optimistic
I hope that the world will let back in with open arms
but until then
I am alone

Our World

David Harlow
7th Grade

It's your world,
treat it as you choose,
treat it well or you might lose.

The Stars

Andrew S. A. Ledezma
4th Grade

The stars are like little lights flashing in the sky.
They're a very beautiful sight.
You could lay and gaze at them all night.
If you really want one
you could fly into outer-space.
You could pick one up and take it home
at a very-very fast pace.

My Ocean

Beth Frey
8th Grade

An endless blue
Deep as a bottom-less pit
Its tide coming in
Going out
The waves crashing upon rocks
Its spray stinging my face
The swells chasing kids along the beach
An exciting memory
A friend who's always there
A soothing lullaby for the troubled soul
An everlasting miracle

The Night Sky Is Beautiful

Emily Audrey Geiszler
3rd Grade

The night sky is beautiful,
enchanting,
and starry.
You can not see the Milky Way
but I bet if we could see it,
it would be beautiful!

Leaves

Amy Daneke
3rd Grade

The leaves falling are like . . .
cold wet raindrops falling from the sky.

The wind carries the leaves
through the air like clouds going back and forth.

The leaves on a summer tree
are like the wet grass on the ground.

Trees are as big as
giant elephants at the circus.

Trees sound like
the wind when I play.

The sunlight through
the trees looks like
the bright lights from heaven.

The Sky at Night

Lauren Sage
7th Grade

As I lay on the crisp, green grass in summer,
I look up at the navy blue sky,
surrounded by stars.
I hear the wind whistle and bugs chirp,
Orion,
Taurus,
Sagittarius,
Gemini and Little Bear.
I look at the moon and see their father smiling.
The Man on the Moon.
The sky is so quiet, it sits still.

Complaining Cat

Heather Huff
6th Grade

My Kitty litter is not right,
I said the litter must be white!
My wind up toy is way too slow,
I want you just to make it go!
My scratching post is way to tall,
Did you do this to make me fall?
But that's O.K.
I guess
I will thank you anyway.

Moon

Eddie Hollenbeck
7th Grade

The moon,
the big sparkly ball in the sky.
The shadow caster
that makes you wonder what's creeping
and crawling and why.
But when I wake up
in the middle of the night
I am comforted
by the light that is shed.

I Am a Wave

Erin Segale
6th Grade

I am a wave
It tickles when people ride me
I love to be big
I love thrashing boats
I am a wave
I hate it when I'm flat
I love big storms
I am free
I like crashing into rocks
I feel cool on people's feet
I am a wave

The Light of the Night

Dustin Leale
7th Grade

The moon,
a silver sphere casting light to the dark side,
casting light not its own.
Shining in the darkest nights
it is the giant center piece of the darkened landscape.
Like a guard shining when the sun cannot.
It catches the light that misses us
and gives it back to our dark night.
Cut into a crescent by the planet it glows for,
but it will keep shining ever more!

Riding Through the Journey of Life

Rachel Allen
6th Grade

Riding through the journey of life,
wondering what each day is going to be like.
Having no fears,
just a whole bunch of tears.
Riding through the journey of life.

Shadow Play

Alex Deleón
7th Grade

We are shadows hiding,
and the moon finds us.

Mouth

Alex Deleón
7th Grade

Water flows into the ocean,
the world's mouth.

Dropped

Alex Deleón
7th Grade

Everyday
the world is picked up
and dropped again.

I Am The Wind

Heather Ross
7th Grade

I am the wind.
I wonder who the new day will blow along beside me.
I hear the bird calls and the sigh as I pass through the trees.
I see everything I could ever want to see,
flowing, blowing, cross the shores.
I want nothing, blissfully nothing,
only to continue on my way.
I am the wind.

I pretend that I can speak to you, whisper in your ear.
I feel only a peaceful calm in the breeze of a cool spring day.
I worry that I can only do so much,
caress the heat of summer, warm the cool of morn.
I cry out in the night with the coming of the storm.
I am the wind.

I understand the clouds,
the way they speak and think and move.
I say the sweet things carried far upon my wings.
I try to feel soft and calm, despite the rush of life today.
I hope to flow on and on,
forever, leading to the stillness of the evening.
I am the wind.

The Polka-Dotted Snake

Heather Ross
7th Grade

My snake is the funniest that can be,
He's covered in polka-dotts for everyone to see.

I am a Raindrop

Cecilia Meza
3rd Grade

I am a raindrop,
I will land in a river,
I see children eating,
I will go swimming,
I will see many creatures,
I cry for my family,
I see something coming, it is my family,
I am so happy,
I am a raindrop.

The Night Sky

Mackenzie Albrecht
3rd Grade

The night sky is dark.
There is fog in the sky.
The moon is like the light
shining down bright.
The moon is in the sky
brightly shining down.
The moon is yawning
and getting very sleepy.

Thing

Clifton Haworth
7th Grade

I saw the strangest thing today,
I don't know what it was,
I'll try to describe it the best I can,
but my brain is in a buzz.
The thing was covered in hot pink dots,
Its' tails were covered with rough ugly knots.
Its' head was made from strawberry jell-o,
Its' tongue was made of a giant marshmallow!
The legs were sticks,
the feet were stones,
and the thing, I think,
did not have bones;
For it wobbled and jiggled, and fell to the ground,
I wonder what it was—this thing that I found.
I really don't know what I saw today.
On this fine afternoon, on the 8th of May.
The thing was HUGE and fluffy,
and fat and ugly,
I saw the strangest thing today—
I don't know what it was!

Trees

Nhu-Anh Le
4th Grade

The wind carries the leaves through the air
like waves in the ocean.
Trees sound like you
when you shiver in the cold wind.
The leaves falling are like raindrops in the sky.
The trees sound like feet stamping on the ground.

Snake

Nhu-Anh Le
4th Grade

A snake feels like scales of a fish.
The skin is as soft as a teddy bear.
Snake colors look like trees.
Luna came to school and ate my homework.
Luna is a boa constrictor.

Night Sun

Elizabeth Avelar
7th Grade

The night sun
is grand, and free
It watches over us
especially me

It brings out the shadows
that have been hiding
It brings calm, and peace
simply watching darkness
begin to fill the earth

It illuminates us
with its glow
It illuminates us
from our world of sorrow,
work, and suffering

And brings us to its pleasurable self
The night sun . . . O yes
The night sun

In My World

Evan White
8th Grade

In my world the air is clean,
the water, crystal clear
the wind, running by my face
I'll always want to hear

In my world, life is great
and pollution never even heard of
where in the sky will always fly
a snowy, sun-white dove

In my world, when oil spills
like a water balloon on a needle
It gets sucked back in from thick to thin
like sunlight on a beetle

Just Look at That Moon

Samantha Baltz
8th Grade

O' my, just look at that moon.
Look at its splendid shine
and its huge and massive power.

Here I sit, just me and this barren tree.
Gazing at the moon.

So big and beautiful, I'd like to reach out and touch it.
The way it's touched me.

The amazing power it holds, binds me like a spell.
My eyes locked on its splendid surface,
so close yet so far away.

I can run but I cannot hide, and I'm glad.
Wow, just look at that moon.

I am Sunshine

Ashley Bielefeld
7th Grade

I am sunshine
I wonder about the darkest clouds
I hear wind whistling
I see smiling faces
I want happiness
I am sunshine

I pretend to be fire
I feel very bright
I worry about wind and rain
I cry about sad people
I am sunshine

I understand people's feelings
I say "I control others"
I try to always stay yellow and orange
I hope never to be darkened
I am sunshine

Snakes

Jeremiah Virgil
7th Grade

Snakes feel like . . .
. . . . well
you'll have to touch one
to find out.

Pollution

Jeremiah Virgil
7th Grade

In my world there's not
much pollution . . . . .
keep it that way!

I Am Mr. Bender's Hair

Thy Nguyen
7th Grade

I am Mr. Bender's hair.
I wonder why he keeps touching me.
I hear many things repeated.
I see a curling iron.
I want to dye myself bright orange.
I am Mr. Bender's hair.

I pretend I don't exist.
I feel sad because I don't belong to someone else.
I worry about dying from gunks of gel.
I cry because I am not like my friends.
I am Mr. Bender's hair.

I understand Mr Bender wants to grow out his hair.
I say things like, "Stop killing me!"
I try to live each day without oxygen.
I hope I don't die from gel and hair spray.
I am Mr. Bender's hair.

In My World . . .

Thy Nguyen
7th Grade

In my world . . . a thick blanket of smoke envelops the sky.
People breathe in hazardous materials,
hoping for clean air once again.
The sun, once radiant, gives off a glow no one can see.
Factories help contribute to the polluted air,
knowing people can die without oxygen.
Outgoing children play inside,
forbidden to step outside and take in the smoke.
In my world . . . everyone lives day by day, once taking
oxygen for granted.

Luna

Katy Stewart
3rd Grade

A snake feels silky.
The skin feels like rubber.
The colors are like a rainbow.
Luna came to school to talk to me.
Luna is my friend.

Shadows

Kelsey Skaggs
6th Grade

In the dark of night
When I'm half sleeping in my bed
I hear the wind howl
Dark shadows creep across the closet
I pull the covers over my head
and hope the shadow monster doesn't hear
how loud my heart is beating
I finally drift into a deep sleep
and wake to the comfort and warmth of the sun

MOONBEAMS

Stephanie Marion
7th Grade

I feel the moon
shining on my face.
If I jump high enough,
I can catch the moon beams,
put them in a jar
and save them for a rainy day.

Snakes

Stephanie Marion
7th Grade

Snakes feel like . . .
a sunbeam on a rainy day

I Fall From The Sky Above

Lauren Ishii
7th Grade

I fall from the sky above.
Gracefully down to Earth.
No one sees me coming.
Never pay attention.
I hit the cold hard ground.
Soak into the moist brown soil.
Wash away, never to be seen again.
I fall from the sky above.

Birch Tree, Spirits and Red Fire

Eric Duskin
6th Grade

While the Birch tree is dazzled with amazement
with its black marks from battles far off.
All is calm in the distant land
where this Birch tree still stands today
in front of the Red Fire warm and cozy
his friends, the spirits keep him company.

Night's Game

Sarah Van Ruiten
8th Grade

I feel lost, engulfed by the darkness.
The crunch of leaves
and essence of the moon's light
makes me shiver with fear.

All alone, with no one to talk to,
I wonder about the previous day
but the outcome is put aside
as the trees sway with delight.

I can no longer think,
for my own mind is whizzing around,
searching for the answers surrounding me.

What was the sound behind me?
Should I turn around to see?
Or will the doubt be enough for conscience to handle?

I giggle at my silliness
as I realize the possibilities.
The moon seems to brighten
as I walk away,
asking me to stay for just a while longer.
The deep colors arouse my inner spirit and I stay,
to play the game with them again.

The Uncurable Pain of Earth

Whitney Sandelin
7th Grade

In my world
doctors can't cure
the pain
of the bad environment.

Untitled

Juan Hernandez
6th Grade

Rain
is like airplanes
thundering
to the ground.
Thunder
is like cymbals
clashing together.
Lightning
is like
the camera's flash.

The Wave

Kevin Taylor
7th Grade

I am a big, blue wave.
I rise high
like a tall building
and feel a surfboard on my back.
I twist and turn
like a big, wet dog and he soon falls off.
Kids scream and try to run away,
but I laugh and knock them over.
People scream and run away,
leaving their fluffy towels on the sandy beach
in front of my raging destruction,
HA HA HA

Flowers

Kiera Hockett
6th Grade

Flowers blooming
look like spring
opening up.

Pollution

Tim Transon
8th Grade

We dropped like flies.
One by one.
Dozens every day.
We had made the worst mistake,
and now we had to pay.
The scientists,
The environmentalists,
no one listened to them cry.
We had polluted our rivers,
And now we were going to die.
We always knew that it was wrong.
But we could never stop.
We covered our land with mounds of trash.
Then put some more on top.
Our throats were parched,
Our skin was cracked,
We were frail and still and dry.
For we had no clean water,
And we all had to die.

In My World . . .

Lauren McGregor
7th Grade

In my world
I can't see the sun
the land is cold and barren
with pollution we did not shun

In my world
children do not play or run
they stay at home
with no clean air, it isn't fun

In my world
the sky isn't blue
the new generation
doesn't believe it was once true

My generation realized
our unfortunate fate
the world isn't perfect
but now it's too late

The Leaves on a Tree

Aj Kahlon
3rd Grade

The wind
carries leaves through the air
like a little tornado.

The leaves
on a summer tree
look like fresh leaves.

Trees
are big
as elephants.

Trees
sound
like rain.

The sunlight
through the trees
looks like orange lights.

I Hear A River

Marcus Shibler
6th Grade

I hear a river
gushing down the rocks and pebbles
It is so quiet
Doing what it does

I hear a river
It makes me feel good inside
I like this river
I hope I come to see it again
I hear a river

Something New

Marcus Shibler
6th Grade

I am an ocean
Going into every crack and crevice I find
Exploring everywhere
Looking for something new

I am an ocean
Playing with the creatures in me
My hands are waves that speed through time
I have been here forever
I look for something new
I think I found something
Yes, I found a treasure
Loving it I do

I Can Talk to the Stars

Aubrey Ramos
4th Grade

I see the stars in the sky
They like to pop out one by one
They're not in a line
I can talk to them
I can have a conversation
I say, "Star Light and stars that are bright
Please do not wake me up
I'm sleeping like the night
I know you work shift to shift
Like a person in the light
But I also say you are fascinating
Like you and I ."
But then they're gone and I say
"See you in the sky on your
next shift
good bye,
good bye!"

Used For the Good

Nick Donn
6th Grade

I am a rain drop that sparkles with radiant beauty.
I was created and combined with others.
I fall, empty silence is achieved.
I fall into one of the veins of the world.
I make an influence.
I am used for the great.
I tell myself, "You will end in the heart of the world."
I drop, swiftly, I pick up speed.
I meet fellow colleagues from the sky.
I stretch my arms with enormous length.
I made it through the pain and violence of the world.
I survived the agony and misery.
I am used, but it is worth it to see
the beauty of the journey of my life.

What is Water Worth?

Mark Ferguson
7th Grade

In my world
water is
as valuable as gold.

The Drop of Rain

Stacie Silva
7th Grade

Falling, Falling, Falling
Down goes the mysterious raindrop until
Pow, it hits the water below
Gently it glides along the smooth river
Floating freely without a care in the world
As it swiftly brushes the sculptured rocks below
Merging with the water it whispers,
It whispers its beautiful song to whoever passes by
Slowly it reaches the open bay
Flowing into the ocean it begins to settle,
Being pulled in and out with the tides,
and hearing the soft cries of the seagulls,
Its journey is finally over,
It is home.

Flying by the Moon

Blair Young
6th Grade

I see birds flying by the moon
I hear them cry out to me to come fly with them
The birds want me to see the moon that is on fire
Then I cry I have no wings so I can fly
The birds then cry and fly,
they fly by the moon that is on fire
I still hear the birds crying to this day

The Moon

Vanessa McDonald
8th Grade

The moon close enough to touch
so close you can taste its essence
and feel its foggy mist
its glowing grace
shines
as it gives off a celestial light
reflected from the sun
imagery
in motion
millions of stars
yet only one
one to be found
a smiling star
connected to the moon
among the millions
I choose one
this single
solitary one
inside the moon's craters
we hide
hide away from the worldly things
I touch the moon
and feel its texture
waiting for one star
among the millions
I am one
you are one
finding each other
two stars in the millions
the moon surrounds us
guides us

to each other
the celestial light draws
us together
the moon
the sun
the stars
combined

A Rain Drop

Tomas Ramirez
7th Grade

A rain drop can be many different things
It can be a fast flowing river
It can be a still and calm pond
It can be a brown muddy puddle
with kids jumping and splashing on it
It can also be a rain cloud
every second getting bigger and bigger
until it becomes a rain drop again
A rain drop can be many different things

I Am a Pair of Glasses

Aprile Fermin
6th Grade

I am a pair of glasses
I wonder how well I help people see
I hear the sound of eye lashes brushing up against my lenses
I see people busily go by a big city
I want to be worn on a special face
I am a pair of glasses

I pretend to see everything
I feel eyes moving along
I worry that I will get shattered
I cry that I won't get to be worn anymore
I am a pair of glasses

I understand I don't see everything
I say to someone, "Don't worry I'll help you see."
I try to help people see better
I hope I will be worn
I am a pair of glasses

Polluted River

Daniel Beseda
7th Grade

I am a sorrowful, distraught river.
I am a river flowing as free as a bird.
Yet I am polluted.
I travel through the rocks,
through moist dirt,
through the moss that lives and grows,
yet I am polluted.
Nothing can change it.
Life is dead and unmeaningful,
the birds no longer visit me,
the fish no longer swim through me.
I am polluted
and it is a horrible thing.

Raining

Michael Miselis
8th Grade

To be a raindrop,
would be living in short bursts.
Free falling through the air.
Living for a few glorious seconds,
then crashing into the Earth.
But always
drying up,
and coming crashing back again.

As I Lay

Amanda Schatz
6th Grade

As I lay
I see the moon
fiery red
like he is mad
at someone
or something
Could it be birds
that wake the moon up
with their hoarse scratchy voices
or could it be the old birch tree
who whistles all night long?
And still today
I wonder
why the moon gets mad?

The Moon, My Friend

Austyn Mahoney
7th Grade

I saw the moon last night
It was so calm
and peaceful
that I told it all my secrets
It was my friend last night
It told me that it wouldn't tell anyone
It was my friend last night

The Moon

Amanda Stoltenberg
6th Grade

It's late in the night,
I climb up a tree,
The higher I get,
It's the moon I see.

It's bright and orange,
With streaks of yellow and red,
I realize it's really late,
And almost time for bed.

But I cannot leave the moon,
It's shining brighter than before,
Now I'm climbing down the tree,
And walking through the door.

Unlikely

Alexandra du Celliée Muller
8th Grade

Look into the sky.
Hey, look!
A flying snake.

Moon-Shadow

Atreese Watkins
8th Grade

I am the moon-shadow
The shadow of the tree
I only come out when
        When the moon is full
        When the sky is clear
        When the night is quiet
        When the people are gone
Other moon-shadows join me sometimes
A lost bird, finding his way up north
A rabbit, restlessly grabbing a moon-night snack
        I am not a shadow, but a spirit
        I was not born here, but there on the moon
It is cleaner up there
where I dare to dream
Where the ground is coated with thick dust
Not red and dirty like here,
But clean, and shining
like the remnants of shattered opals
        The sidewalks are platinum,
        The sun-people know this and they envy us
        All is music, I like to dance
        But sometimes I come to earth
                When the moon is full
                When the sky is clear
                When the night is quiet
                When the people are gone
And I rest in the grass
And I listen to the wind calling me

Moon-Shadow

The Stars

Andrew Moses
6th Grade

The stars are very important I feel,
because they are like the guardians of day,
and protectors of night.
They hover in the night above,
they sail in the day just like a glove.
They protect our hands,
our body,
our soul.
So you see the stars are very important
or at least I think so.

Snakes

Andrew Moses
6th Grade

Snakes are like moving twigs on the ground,
moving all around.
Snake scales feel like
putting your hand on the surface of water
in the summer, so cool, so soothing.
Snake scales are petite,
so small and round.

The Moon

Steven Ofenham
5th Grade

The moon
is like a diamond
that shines
brightly each night.

The moon
is like a flashlight
that is left on
all night.

The moon
is like an eye
watching ever
so closely.

The moon
is just like a friend
that is
always watching.

Snakes

Caira Vanderveen
6th Grade

Boas are long and fluid.
Corn snakes are calm and morbid.
Gophers are fast and hide.
Milk snakes are red as blood.
Snakes are wonderful.
Snakes are strong.
Snakes are all tail and very long!

Night

Kayla Bobrow
5th Grade

I stare
deeply into the midnight sky.
It's as quiet
as an angel baby sleeping.
The only thing I can hear
is the lively dance of the crickets.
Stars are very tiny diamonds.
Out in the open is where I gaze.

Jewel of The Valley

A California Anthology

J. Jackson Harvey
Editor

Special Thanks to Betsy Lee . . . For the cover
A photograph of a reflection on the wall of the
All Veterans Plaza in Lodi California.

Sponsored in part by a grant from

Lodi Arts
COMMISSION

Forward . . .

Surrounded by night, outside my home in Lodi, California, I stand looking at the sky and drinking in its grander and brilliance. Slowly I become aware of the thought, "*What makes this beautiful is, where I am.*" Living in the San Joaquin valley, one of the most productive, fertile areas of the world, I am surrounded by fruit trees, vineyards, and agriculture of all sorts. It is a valley of rare beauty and productivity. Is it any wonder the moon hanging in the sky is our nocturnal partner, that the stars blinking in the sky are fellow travelers, that the night inspires poetry?

No wonder the San Joaquin valley is a touchstone for poets and writers, artists and musicians, singers and dancers. It is out of this sense of creative wonder that the poetry in this book reflects the works of poets who have given a great deal of beauty, life and hope to the people of this valley.

This book, *Jewel of the Valley* is an anthology produced by Blue Moon Press and sponsored by the Lodi Arts Commission.

The *Jewel of the Valley Poetry Series* monthly show has had a number of extraordinary poets come and read their works over the past two years. This collection features many of those poets.

Poetry is a spiritual language and connects us to ourselves and to each other as jewels in the crown of human experience in the context of the world in which we live.

Taking Communion Again

The moon,
a white disk against the night,
a wafer of the holiest sort,
like the Eucharist of the Universe
handed out before the altar of time.
I stand in awe—mouth open
waiting to receive.
Every full moon is the same,
a moment of spiritual ritual
against the face of eternity,
both yours and mine.

Jim Harvey
Editor

Table of Contents

James Lee Jobe, a radio DJ in Sacramento, has three chapbooks published. For five years he served as the editor of One Dog Press, a poetry monthly. He lives in Davis with his wife and children. His poetry and presence have long been a part of the Northern California arts community.

Chapters of my Magical Life

James Lee Jobe

I climbed into this poor body to write poems.
It's a chore, living this life, a spirit inside of flesh,
struggling in this world.

Spirits know, but bodies feel.
Guess which a poet needs most!
Without a body you can't feel poetry, much less write it.

Perhaps we come here, knowing it all ahead of time,
every pain and anguish, but we chose to come anyway;
needing to feel.

Of course we forget all that when we step into the body.
We don't know anything then! Not even where the poems go!

Poems put into anthologies die, it's too cold there,
Rumi said that.
Poems spoken aloud rise up to some other world,
invisible, a mist!

Some people seem overly concerned with
where poems come from.
They write impressive papers on the subject,
but I don't care.

How many of these poems are chapters of my magical life?

Little invisible books? Read aloud by elves or other beings?

You may have noticed by now;
I'm no Albert Schweitzer. I don't care how you live,
or if you have something to do. That's your problem.

Everybody Wins at
Old Blue Jay's Morning Shower

James Lee Jobe

I like to wait until the last cool edge of morning to water our old lemon tree,
and when I do Old Blue Jay stops down for a late morning shower. A sly and

attentive bird, Old Blue Jay has learned the rhythm of our water sprinkler.
When the spray lands on our lemon tree, or on our peach tree, which are

away from the house, Old Blue Jay lands for a moment right in the cold spray,
preens and grooms like its his wedding day, and stretches as if he's doing tai chi.

When the spray flips over to the house, Old Blue Jay flits up to the fence top,
checking security, and waiting for the spray's return. In this manner, Old Blue Jay

eventually gets his full shower, our trees and lawn get a much needed drink,
I get this marvelous entertainment and maybe a poem.
Everybody wins.

WHAT I SAID WHEN COYOTE ASKED ME WHAT MAGIC IS

James Lee Jobe

It is hot on this trail; Magic is water- (I tell him)
Magic is the breeze blowing cool on your face
and helping the trees to do a windy dance
That meadow lark song? Hear it? That's Magic
if you hear it from beginning to end
(It’s like listening to the First Bird!)
Magic is being questioned by an old fool like you
on this hot trail - Stand aside, Damn Fool Coyote!
I have two more miles to hike to Stoddard Lake.

Betsy Lee is the President of Blue Moon Press, co-host of the Jewel of the Valley Poetry Series. She works as an artist in residence for California Poets in the Schools. She lives in Lodi, California with her husband, Jim Harvey, their children and an eight foot boa named Luna. Ms. Lee's paintings and poetry are well known. She is published in two books, *The Best of Blue Moon Press* and *Whispers Along The Delta*. She has a number of chapbooks including, *Sycamore Street* and *Family, Family and Family*. One of her poems is etched in granite at the All Veteran's Plaza in Lodi, California.

Knowing What I NOW Know

Betsy Lee

If I were twenty . . .
or maybe twenty two
I would wear my hair in dread locks
long and tangled
maybe die it blue, or pink, or even bright red

If I were twenty . . .
now, instead of then
I would read my poetry on a street corner
in Berkeley, all the while drinking my Latté
with dread locks in my hair
maybe died pink or blue, black
or bright red

If I were twenty . . . NOW
I would have a few more tattoos
art expressing where I had been in my few short twenty years
or where I was going
maybe one about who I wasn't . . . just to confuse
contrary to those who's tattoos

tell something about themselves
all the while I would
read my poetry on a street corner
maybe in a café
in Berkeley, drinking my Latté
with bright red dread locks in my hair
or maybe black or blue but definitely not graying

If I were twenty . . .
and knew, what I NOW know
I am sure I would do things different
time gives perspective that can not be erased
maybe I would slip through the cracks
and start a software business
or a publishing company for young poets like myself
or go to college
or just fly off to The Florida Keys
with dread locks in my hair
maybe died pink or blue, black or bright red
and I would read my poetry
where ever I went
even on a street corner or in a small café
thinking about
writing about
reading who I would become
when I was forty four

Death Comfort

Betsy Lee

sometimes this woman
walks through graveyards
reads the names
among the shadows

reads the dates
among the stone markers
reads between the lines
wonders
about people she will never know
those who lay below her

somehow it is comforting
surrounded by death
the silence
the green grass
the tall trees
the woman feels more alive
among the dead

this woman knows time will
take those she loves away
and the woman
will walk
through graveyards differently

This Woman

Betsy Lee

This woman sits and listens
to the words of poets
who hang their tainted feelings
over the ears of those who choose to listen
like a wet deer skin
freshly removed from the meat laden corpse

This woman hears
the smell of their poetic anger

and their passion for mortal life
and their poetic rectitude
these nails hold the skin in place
on the tanning board

This woman
can hold near the fallen sparrow
who has tried flight way before its wings were ready
can toss away old lover's words
as if wiping away a passage of her life were possible
can rest within the pages of her book of life,
her written poetry,
when the world becomes too large
and hunting is insufferable

Look At This Boy

Betsy Lee

look at this boy
with his fifteen and a half year old face
pimply
dotted with innocent youth
rounded features
this is my son
my last son
one of two, cherished sons

look at this boy
who wants with all his might
to be nobody
to blend into the crowd unnoticed
to disappear among his peers
though I see him as being somebody
somehow
someday

look at this boy
who still dresses up in Knight's clothes
and plays with his Mullet friend
in the yard
with sticks and broken metal swords . . . pretending
to be great
and truthful
wise
and noble

look at this boy
who soon . . . will be a man
and will have to give up playing
and will have to be responsible
and will have to hold a job
and make money
and find a house to live in
and know pain
and know love

and know the things
I now know
as I watch him in the yard
and wonder what it would feel like
to once again
dress up in Knight's clothes?

Melanie Bishop Sievers work has appeared in many publications. She also assembles performance pieces that are "almost plays" and publishes small edition artist-made books under Jump and Shout Publications. www.jumpandshout.com

Spring Fever

for Joyous Young Men - Jack, Mike, Steve

Melanie Bishop Sievers

When lilacs last in the dooryard bloomed,
I did, too.
After winter's pale, purple moods
Heidelberg in April and a young girl in bud
grew fragrant and heady
in the heat of spring.

I've borrowed some lines from male poets
who stepped out of their bodies, not in
to get their juices to flow,
as I've borrowed from men all my life,
stealing their clothes and their aftershave,
learning their ways.
I was called Jimmy awhile at age five
so I could borrow the joy of the men in my
life,
so I could steal my father's laugh,
my brother's grin
and throw back my head and whistle
and shake Nehi's to make them explode
camp in a pup tent and catch tadpoles,
and brag.
In Heidelberg, that spring,
I didn't want to steal or to borrow.
I wanted a gift.
I played in the park and waited
for joyous young men to come in,
to find me by smell, I suppose,
to show me their maleness,
to show me their difference.
I wanted to take their joy into my body
and I with it.

Winters and winters since then,
I banked up my pride with the snow
and built up my dignity,
one indignity at a time.
As my men lost their mirth and I lost my
youth,
through winters and winters
I've waited for spring.

Thank You Note

Melanie Bishop Sievers

Becoming superfluous again
hurts again
if I let myself listen
(beneath the stiff, embarrassed courtesies
and the clank of washing dishes)
to my heart's little chirping cries
like the rhythmic clinking sound
of the turning
fans that cools us not at all.

I gather up my optimism
along with my diaphragm and lipstick
and you empty ashtrays
and strip sheets off the bed
so I don't stink up your tidy life
with my extraneous love.

Gratitude wears off
like your cologne. The scent
that seemed so deep as I sprayed
you into my suitcase
evaporates
in the heat of day
leaving only the bitter odor
of your dismissal and my grief.

Heather Hutcheson is a creative writing and composition instructor with the Los Rios Community College District. Heather spends the majority of her time outside the office working to promote the arts in Sacramento. She is Managing Editor of Poetry Now, Sacramento's only literary review and calendar.

off stage

Heather Hutcheson

the one wearing all white surrenders all
of her attention to the man on her
left, another madly sketches
me & another
sketches her in her rendering
of my plain reading
from my first chapbook, really
a journal that seems suddenly like a great
marble sarcophagus
& the man at the far right,
in the front row, who barely hears me
whinny like the fantastic horse
that broke from her pasture & ran
alongside the crowded middle-school bus
spends his attention
on the derivation of *sarcophagus*
form the Greek, "flesh-eating stone,"
how when you open it up years later,
the coffin or the fledgling chapbook,
with the photograph of early summer
arrived in the pasture, the brilliant green
dissolved itself & is the greedy man
on the aisle, his fingers wagging
with want; demands I lean closer
into the mic, be more . . . & next to him
another man giggles at every end
stop; they cannot know how I arrived
in front of them, almost mad
with worry for what they might recognize
in my words.

Honey

Heather Hutcheson

The friend gets married by the lake
in another state & the woman is there
to count the minutes of the ceremony:12;
the bees:7,003: & the other friends: three
dozen dressed in black & four in spring
pinks.

The woman has come to give her
blessing, to check out the new man,
to watch the circus between the two
families, to meet the strange cousin
who was shot while defending Domino's
from some hungry person back in the 80's
& laughs about it now, how patriotic
he'd been to the company, even had a "D"
shaved into the back of his hair.

The friend is pregnant, due soon
after the honeymoon & forgets her vows
& cusses at the extinguished unity candle &
cusses to the wind that blows it out
a fourth time. The woman promises herself
that she will carry the story back to friends
with a title insisting: radiance, celebration,
longevity. She will fill in the middle
with lines from poems she's wanted to write:

The man saw her and thought: wild
flowers: larkspur, white yarrow, evening
primrose, dame's rocket. He offered her
a quiet audience for beauty, knew her
like summer and winter stars, like books

The woman will become one of the bees, lifting,
bearing only the nectar of the afternoon.

Frank Andrick is the poet behind the press, that is AMP Press, which he operates with John Thomas Mead. He has his own radio poetry show in San Francisco and is famous for his part in the fabulous Three Poets Tour.

Fragments

Frank Andrick

I do not believe that ignorance is bliss
I believe that ignorance is ignorance
And i wish i could tear the root out of that word
IGNORE.

A living death sentence is
The knowledge that my many flaws
Will keep me from what i want most.

Paradigm of integrity; A person
Without a price is a prince without a country
Who inhabits interior landscapes that know
No End.
This is the price of integrity
An engaging onslaught of images.

Remember - The place where the eyes
Stop short - Is where the vision begins.

Assuming credit for doing good is not
to far removed from doing evil.

Illuminata - Illuminatrix

(excerpts)
Frank Andrick

Illuminata - Illuminatrix

Notre Dame du Lumiere
Notre Dame du Souterrian
Notre Dame du Grace

Our Lady of Light
Our Lady of The Underworld
Our Lady of Grace

Look at her
she looks like she knows how to
swarm and splinter into the
dreams all around her.

Only Modigliani
could begin to distill her essence
into line
and to that she would always offer more
in accordance to her natures
surpassing everywhere and everything.

A beauty with no bounds
unchanged by time
untouched by decay
In that shining
the rapture of communion
as only the unknown can know
in and of itself
That answers only to itself
In language of colour, sound and heat
Hearts On Fire

Always the sum of your many faces.

Illuminata - Illuminatrix

(excerpts)

Path, the dual sexed god
who beghat the rest
both god and goddess

Sekmet
Lion girl beyond the world
born from the blood that dropped from
the eye
blood that turned to ghost
when it splashed across the sand
That blood still burns and vanishes into the
eyes of the women I look into.

I remember those times
of Sekmit and Bast
the lioness and the cat
I still bear the scars of the night
beside the Nile
And even now in a mirror capture
the fleeting glimpse of rivelets and ribbons
of the spirit
of the flesh
and then gone as the new flesh
replaces memory . . . and a lifetime floods
The dream

Bast, the Cat
the nurture that prepares the soul
for emergence into life and
it's subsequent escape into light.
Isis, Ishtar, and I
All one and the same
by a different name.

Illuminata - Illuminatrix
(excerpts)

Infinity and Eternity
Cast inwards like a searchlight
probing the hidden heart
It sears, I hurt
It sears, I hurt

A lonely alchemist caught in the great divide
a black crow with a white head
kill the great raven
and the green lion,
that egg enwrapped by a snake
I know you all to well
I've seen you in my dreams

In Dantes hell
Satan was imprisoned to his thighs
by a burning ice
In Vahthec by William Beckford
The heart flames in pain
entombed in ice like glass
so you can watch it burn.

I do not remember when it did not burn
I cannot remember when it did not burn
It Burns.
Then a cool wind filled with kisses
blows away the ash.

Jim Harvey is a Lodi poet, writer, columnist, minister, arts commissioner and he co-hosted the Jewel of the Valley poetry series in 2001. He has two books of poetry published and seven chapbooks. For more than a decade he has served as an instructor for Dynamic Communicator's International. He is also involved in a continuing love affair with the High Sierras.

A Fourth of My Life Is in Sleep

Jim Harvey

1.
I dream of Langston Hughes looking at our world
here at the end of the age and weeping for it.
2.
I dream that my hands have remained young
while the rest of my body has aged alone.
3.
I dream the University of Alabama has a losing football team and
the rest of the world cheers anyway.
4.
I dream the islands of the Pacific Ocean
are encased in ice and all the dancers are frozen.
5.
I dream a woman with dark eyes has stepped out of the forest and
beckons us to follow her into the night.
6.
I dream that Jesus Christ stands on Bayshore Drive
calling out to the passing cars in Spanish, "Bienvenida!
Bienvenida!"
7.
I dream I catch my mother smoking marijuana,
my wife wonders how I can laugh in my sleep.
8.
I dream the child picked last for softball
does not feel the pain of being last.
9.
I dream a woman in her fifties
still thinks about her life in terms of hope.

10.
I dream the car I am driving
is slowing down and I can't seem to make it go any faster.
11.
I dream the sun rises over the Dome of the Rock
and the air is quiet and no one is moving.
12.
I dream of violent death in Southeast Asia
men and women struggling to survive without scars.
13.
I dream I am talking to Henri Nouwen but he is distracted by the
paintings surrounding us in the Louve
14.
I dream Jack Gallagher is giving ice cream to everyone,
it makes the world a better place.
15.
I dream of young love as it was meant to be
soft, innocent and without fear.
16.
I dream I am standing in front of a mirror,
is it a man? Is it a woman? Who knows.
17.
I dream of Joe Montoya saying over and over again, "Hey, Mr.
Hall of Famer, who do you think you are talking to?"
18.
I dream of a man walking on a crowded beach
stepping over bodies, some sunburned, some not.
19.
I dream of my daughter when she was a baby,
my eyes drink deeply of her child's face.
20.
I dream Peter Jennings is telling about the wolves
that have invaded downtown L.A. He is afraid.
21.
I dream the world is bathed in tragedy and war,
and wake up crying to find it is the truth.
22.
I dream the pope is jogging beside me,
his voice praying strangely in a foreign tongue.

23.
I dream of a fourteen year old boy alone,
the wonder of his own life unfolding before him.
24.
I dream of a man standing at a bus stop
the smoke of his cigarette drifting into the night.
25.
I dream of musicians pounding out rock and roll
the young girls before them dance with abandon.
26.
I dream I'm standing at Dallas' Daily Plaza
the tears of a nation stream endlessly down our faces.
27.
I dream the wind blowing in the maple trees,
the sound takes on a texture of sorrow.
28.
I dream a young John Lennon walking past Chapman,
An almond eyed woman is screaming a warning, it is too late.
29.
I dream I am knocking on my grandmother's door,
when she opens it, it startles me because she looks so young.
30.
I dream, long, strange, and erotic dreams
that always leave me uncertain and guilty.
31.
I dream of the steam rising off the Niagara River
a woman is standing on the wall waiting to jump.
32.
I dream of a dark skinned woman with violet eyes
she looks down into a crib but the child is gone.
34.
I dream I am again in Catholic school surrounded by taller
students in dark uniforms and closed eyes.
35.
I dream I am a guest on the Ricki Lake show,
the more I try to talk, the less I am understood.
36.
I dream of a woman swimming away from me,
I can not tell what she is wearing but it is enticing.

37.
I dream Sandi Wasserman is sitting at my breakfast table,
I am unnerved about what to say to her.
38.
I dream I am walking into my high school gym.
Once again I am alone in a sea of strangers.
39.
I dream of a world where truth is a lie,
the lies are embraced by everyone in the name of honesty.
40.
I dream of my poetry, read and unread, a lifetime of words,
unborn and unspoken, waiting to be said.
41.
I dream of the year two thousand and ten, a poet standing alone,
Langston Hughes, still crying for everything and everyone.
I dream a world.

Monticello

Jim Harvey
"The Apron That is My Mother"
-Nancy Wallace - February 17, 2002
Third Sunday Writing Group

She is ninety-four,
her life has spiraled down
to medications, mass and meals.

Everything else is the outside world,
Everything else is a distant memory,
Everything else is what used to be,
it no longer touches or reaches
it no longer is important
it no longer is worth noting,
but still,
in the quiet of early mornings
when I find her asleep in her chair,
up early

because time is her only companion
up early
because time is the night's softest touch
up early
because time is a fog in the high Sierras
up early
because time is a mist against the Everglades
up early
because time is a whispering breeze against
the window pane.

She turns her aged face,
with it's paper thin skin
with it's thick glasses and failing eyes
with it's lost look of wonder
of who she once was,
what she vaguely remembers
what still speaks out her past life.
She turns her face
towards me and smiles,
"Ah," she says,
like the lines of a long remembered poem,
like the words of favorite novel,
like the dialogue in a medieval play,

"Ah," she says,
like an often repeated mantra,
like a blessing from a prayer,
like a priestly benediction,
"Ah," she says,
"you were always such a sweet boy."

She remembers nothing,
I remember everything,
we are so far apart,
we are so close.

Three Haikus for Winter
Jim Harvey

Winter
The sun moves slowly,
a woman leaving a man,
cold and shorter days

Winter
Without a warning
the cold wind breathes frozen night
against your window

Winter
Winter, without heart
takes the warmth from your sky
alone, cold, helpless

Two Cities
Jim Harvey

The sky is too blue,
the wind too cold.
Buildings rise beyond my eyes
until I can no longer see them.
They disappear into the brilliant sky.

The bay is so bright,
the water so blue.
Ships sail beyond my eyes
until I can no longer see them.
They disappear into the dazzling sea.

The air is too cool,
the smells too strong.

People fill the space beyond my eyes
until I can no longer see them.
They disappear into the shining city.

No matter how many times,
it always seems like the first time,
the best time, the last time, the only time,
San Francisco.

* * * * * * * *

Arriving at the airport
I am overwhelmed,
an avalanche of people,
dark skinned and
dark haired,
beautiful beyond belief
surround me.

I am drowning in sounds.
Spanish flows around me
like the warm water
on a summer beach.

I close my eyes
drink in the wonder
of a nation,
a people,
a culture
deeply spiritual
yet, powerfully human.

I am always in a swirl of faces,
I am surrounded by sounds,
enveloped in smells,
encircled by the exotic.

Sometimes I fly here
just to be baptized by
Mexico City.

Maliger, aka **Donald Anderson** is a regular reader of poetry in the Stockton, California area. He is a past winner of a Stockton Poetry Contest in the area of spiritual poetry.

Blue.11.06.2001

Maliger

A sphere
solid bluity
in the fire
it lathers
contained
a world
a teardrop
an emotion
furthest from her mind.
Where does the blue lie?
It is meant to truth.
It does not lie.
Where does the blue lay?
It does not lay.
It settles.
It celebrates.
It celebrates in celibacy.
Where does the blue live?
It is distant.
She can't see it.
She never has.
All she knows is the
orange flame,
which consumes it,
and she opens her mouth,
and the flame comes from
within her.
Chandelier light?
No.
Forest fire?
No.
Sun's furnace?
No.
Hell?
No.
The Big Bang?
No.
What about flicker
that you see
just before falling asleep?
No, because
each is an individual fire,
and
her flame
has drowned the blue.

Faith Parizo Harper is a social studies teacher at Tokay High School. She has lived in Lodi for the last 18 years after moving here from Ohio with her two children. Active in many organizations, she welcomes new experiences to express herself.

WHITE UNDERWEAR

Faith Parizo Harper

I will wear white underwear now
White cotton underwear
Perhaps a size too large
So that my bellybutton is covered
Bunching on the sides and back
Thick enough to be seen
When I wear slacks.

I will wear faded flannel thermals in the winter
Insulated from head to toe
Sterile, white nurse's bras will gird
Up my desires.

I will wear cotton muu-muus in the summer
Blousey enough
Billowing around my figure
Frousy enough to turn no man's head.

And I will put on just enough weight
To pad myself
into a girdle
that I can refuse to wear.

Now I know what a Hope Chest is for

Now I know what to keep
(Hidden) in my lingerie drawer
. . . until you leave.

Adrienne Reynolds is a student at Elkhorn School in North Stockton, California. She wrote poetry as a part of classroom work and then came to read at the show.

If It Weren't For You Cat

Adrienne Reynolds

If it weren't for you, cat,
I would not have to chase you;

If it weren't for you, cat,
I wouldn't have to feed you;

If it weren't for you, cat,
I wouldn't have to move things;

If it weren't for you, cat,
I could play with my friends;

If it weren't for you, cat,
I could rest without you meowing;

If it weren't for you, cat,
I could eat my food in peace;

If it weren't for you, cat,
I could stop putting you in the garage;

But if it weren't for you, cat,
I would miss your soft fur.

Untitled

Adreinne Reynolds

First the two and then the three;
First the hive and then the bee.
First things first.

First the heart and then the ribs;
First the baby and then the bibs.
First things first.

First the thigh and then the knee;
That's the way it had to be.
First things first.

Alan N. Satow has been active in the Stockton, California poetry scene for a long time, reading in many venues including Stockton's Annual First Night Show. He is the last of the Neo-Goths.

Last Poem On Earth

Alan N. Satow

Everything is now gone and forgotten.
Fear rules the land, once more.

Entering the new city
the light / fire hits the towers—
slanting from the hour.

The ground vibrates in sun.

You didn't awaken
until it was too late.

It was warm enough to
walk without a coat.

On the street of
stocks, gold and dreams of riches.

You say, take a picture.

I just scream:
a silver bird
small curling and
diving.

You run around with a video camera—
taking pictures—in delight—

that the world—never seen before.

So many passageways of lives
following the STREET . . .
Where everything has decided to live
It will live.

This is a story, this time now.

Her hand struck out of the rumble,
waiting for Jesus.

Pale flesh, I know.

The soul, pushed about in the dirt and debris.

Finally stepping out.

Preparing this, for a long time.

In writing;
don't what to do. Pain and suffering.

Seeing the cross from the ashes.

Waiting for the visions to leave.
While living today.
Alternate lives.
Still petrified!

The unknown took me, yet I should
have know.

En Spiritus, Spiritus yenal.
Smooth comfort, grasping for breath.

Erin Biskup is twenty-six year old poet from Sacramento California. Her work appears in *The Best of Blue Moon Press.* She is active in the renaissance movement. *"Her majesty's a pretty nice girl but she doesn't have a lot to say . . . Her Majesty's a pretty nice girl but she changes from day to day . . . I wanna tell her that I love her a lot . . ."*

The Beatles

Moments

Erin Biskup

There are moments that change a person.
The birth of a child, the death of a parent.
There are moments that change a family,
Finding the perfect home, losing a family pet.

There are moments that change a community.
The end of a difficult election, the closing of a factory.
There are moments that change a nation.
The destruction of an icon, the loss of so many lives.

Time passes, memories dull, but are never really forgotten.
Time passes, hearts heal, but scars always remain.
Time passes, buildings are restored, but others are gone forever.
Time passes, a nation returns to life, but nothing is really the same.

People crawl out from under the terrifying images of tragedy.
People dust the debris of hatred from their souls.
People take their first steps towards the light of normality.
People pack their camouflage bags and prepare to defend liberty.

We turn on the television and see the messages from home.
We turn on the television and see the images of war.
We turn on the television and see the tribute songs.
We turn on the television and see the pictures of Ground Zero.

But what happens next?

We wait. We wait. We wait. We wait.

There are moments that change a person.
There are moments that change a family.
There are moments that change a community.
There are moments that change a nation.

And those moments never change.

Joe Montoya is the long time host of *Poetry Unplugged*, a Sacramento institution for poetry reading. He has produced a numbers of books and shows, and has toured California as a part of the *Three Poets Tour*.

Adios, Fidel

Joe Montoya

I wrote in the book of life today
so long, Fidel. You didn't want to
hurt us but we could not feel
your pain. Now the Angel of
Eternity holds you in her arms.
We said farewell to you Fidel but
how we remember the comfort in
your every hello. It wasn't your
fault you did not hear us and the
light in our life grew dimmer today.
We reached to understand the cruelty
of depression in its unreserved grip.
I wrote in the book God speed Fidel,
and your family will always feel
the glow in your voice and the glimmer
of your kind eyes. I wish we
could have risen above the hurdle of
silent terror with you. I wrote in the
book today because the God of
forgiveness awaits in the hallway of
your desperate plea. Today we cried
in your memory hoping that life was
more than a cruel method. We
asked for mercy Fidel, and longed
for a day we never had to say
adios, again.

Written in honor of my Uncle Fidel

November 18, 1975 (tribute to Cesar Chavez)

Joe Montoya

Cesar, you felt the pain of
my Grandpa Sal in Fowler and
picked up the pieces of ripened
deflection in Cutler. You spoke
for the silent and knew how
piercing cold injures the soul.
The enemy prefers the higher
ground but your warmth was the
depth of the poor. Your words
unwrapped the corpse of the
farm worker where they lay.
The hunger in your heart fed the
family in Sanger and the calm
in your voice was the scream
for justice in the fields of a
summer weep. The immensity
of your belief was the embrace
of its force and healing
was your remedy. As I submerged in
my deathbed on that cold winter
night you stopped to write me a
letter, just to say you were sorry.
That letter, dated 11/18/75 hangs
on my wall and I touch it every day
for the mending that it brought
to my mother . . .
and my dad . . . and my sister . . .
and my brothers . . . and
because the words
were written for everyone.
By the grace of God I survived
to live in a better world
because of you.

Jose f. Cantu is the author of one book of poetry, *Vale of Dreams*. He continues to write traditional verse and resides in Stockton, California.

Stopping In Palo Duro

Jose f. Cantu

Abuelito led the burro,
as they stumbled along the pass.
On the burro sat Arturo,
negotiating the crevasse.

Soon, a criticism was heard,
when someone concurrently said,
"that is absolutely absurd.
Abuelo should ride, nieto tread."

On hearing the criticism,
the two then quickly changed places.
Abuelo rode through the chasm;
Arturo smiled in good graces.

Shortly, one more complaint was noised,
"Why, that miserly Abuelo.
Has he no shame to sit so poised?
The boy should ride this camino!"

Hearing that, old Abuelo stopped,
helped Arturo on the burro;
so that they could both ride atop,
through the final mountain furrow.

Soon, another censure arose,
“Look at that,” a voice pierced the air;
“Don’t they feel the pack burro’s woes?”
They thus got off and left him bare.

Abuelo and Arturo then,
carried the little pack burro
on their shoulders with strength of ten;
till stopping in Palo Duro.

You see, no matter what you do,
someone will ever criticize.
Whether lead, ride or transport too,
some will always seek to chastise.

Teresa Ansani moved from the Bay Area to the Central Valley in 2000. She is an avid hiker and spends many hours in the mountains and along the seashore. It's here she is most inspired.

Silent Self

Teresa Ansani

Crushed, broken, pounded and dispersed
are the idiosyncracies, doubts and
insecurities

Out from the cocoon emerges self—
the delicate winged thing,
gently unfolding wings wet with
newness.

Exposing self to the sun.

Self—Some tried to crush and crunch
the cocoon from which self grew silently.

Silence—In the silence, in the womb,
in the warmth of the cocoon
was security.

Some came and tired to rock it
away.
Still, Life—force persisted and
protected and guarded it each
day.

In the protected covering self
persisted, until at last its spirit
strengthened . . . and it emerged!

The beautiful butterfly in you,
the beautiful butterfly in me.

Each creation is a solemn
Song to Creator . . .
a praise.
Each lovely soul with
wings and heart raised . . .

Sing joyfully for
each of us is
Unique.

Ron Houssaye is founding member of the San Leandro Poets' Society. A Bay Area poet supplanted in The Valley, he is a social worker for a private social service agency.

Homage

Ron Houssaye

Let us toast the poets put lately to rest,
Lay leaves of their poems across their biers.
Enduring scorn, and savaged by storms within,
They stiffened our courage that much more.
Eliot sang of the Hollow Men,
While cummings purposely failed to punctuate.
Whitman penned his Leaves of Grass in love,
And his Democratic Vistas emboldened our nation.
Emily Dickenson, the Belle of Amhearst,
Shut out the world to find truth in her verses,
Resigning her soul to poetry's contentment.
Countee Cullen, that noble heart, poetized human rights,
Proclaiming his people not merely free, but royal.
Hart Crane's father disapproved of him
Yet his poetry "held him together" to the end.
Dear Anne Sexton painfully testified about an inner war
Within her psyche, for us all to behold.
On and on, they strove to translate wordless intuitions
Fashioning word structures of truth and beauty
And manifested in verse humanity's vast and bodiless wonder.
Let them receive the thanks of our hearts.

Paula Sheil is a staff writer for the Stockton Record and the editor of ZamBamba, a San Joaquin Valley poetry journal. Ms. Sheil has won numerous awards and been recognized by Stockton for her work in the arts.

On What Is Writing

Paula Sheil

Sentences that allow themselves to be herded into paragraphs tend to become their own trap.

Ideas carried on their heads in rainbow bundles burn brightly, swiftly, and are extinguished like fireworks in the summer sky.

All that's left are the thin ash shreds on the cold white page. And silence.

Why am I here, you ask? Trapped in these rows of single lines. What grew here? There is no past. No future.

You start to imagine your seed is worth money. And money has brought you all the color life prints each dawn on the new negative.

So you pump the handle in front of your body in an iron well grip, and before you know you are thirsty (or parched white like the page), coins, golden and silver clank melodiously from your saving up, and bury their heads in the chocolate silt.

How proud you are to spend your fortune reviving this tale.

When you have waited a sufficiently long time for change and the paragraph refuses to show you new thoughts, you abandon hope, yourself and purpose. There never was a point. I told

you it was a trap. And yet you tied yourself up in commas and periods, breathing hard, swallowing and stopping, for what?

Let's say you decide to withhold your desire. Standing tall in a desperate landscape, you instead whistle for stars and work your toes in the fleshy dirt. Now there is a top to bottom as well as left to right, but you're still trapped, holding this thought.

And only when your bones leak all their calcium and the multitudes of vagrant beetles chew the flesh from your palms, does your whistle thread an echo back.

And the stars cover you like a blanket shrinking.

Maybe instead a long lost girlfriend from high school appears drifting by on clouds like Helen on a grand divan. You think there is color: red, purple possibly, or maybe orange, but there's deceit.

Now even memory can no longer manufacture those prismatic waves. They are jokes without punch lines.

Seeds germinating in their own white packets in the gardening shed. When your dream girl floats from view, you think you remember violet and you taste salt.

I brought you to this page to help me. Many times I've held a compass to these lines and found no direction. I can't reverse myself or support the sky on my shoulders any more than I can breathe the blackness into my lungs or digest earth's flesh like the worm.

I keep making these traps and falling in.
And falling out.

And inviting you to wait with me.
And sending you away.

Who Says There Are Stars?

Paula Sheil

I defy you. Stars. Romeo said that.
Apocalyptic. The moon rests.
The heart hung.
How gold thy cloth girds our pleasure.
In food. Incense.
And pleasant confessions.
How piano my nerves.
How bag creaking, glass clinking, the kitchen
calls after dinner. San Francisco.
Clean blue baby day in an open car.
You. A cat. Smoking. My love, a lavender
field hence. A dream waking and held long enough to be
written.
Be palms. Your moons in my hands. So be it.
This, my city music box.
Wish you were melting chocolate, afternoon.
You sigh. The wind brushes dry the winter cliffs.
Hard rains.
The wind again.
You right.
Your hand upon mine. And breath parts sorrows.
How you look. Questions. All mine as well.
My hands reach and fill.
Imagining. And literate night comes to mind. To me.
Like a trust. Green and red.
So not solstice,
winter's shortest sun.
But decayed.
Past prime. Your whole song singing low octaves.

Your dive sounding.
My oceans.
Back and forth like a jay. Not a stellar, no croaking
                                        beggary.

You a mountain blue, perhaps.
                        High twig grappling, an open,
                              no oxygen and sun burn.

How it is in high altitudes. Tender.
Geese flying overhead.   Swans following.
And Monarchs.

How tender do you need it?

Nancy Wallace grew up in the Great Lakes region and moved to California from Canada. Her work has been in many publications including *Poetry Now, Blue Moon Quarterly* and in a book, *Whispers Along The Delta.* She has a passion for playing classical piano. She is a treasure for poets everywhere and remains the Queen of Hearts.

for Loree

Nancy Wallace

four little girls (perhaps) started out together

and at first everything fit on a meadow

which had an interesting hollow on certain afternoons

revisited in later winter reveries

but as the years went by and the money flowed in

the reveries stopped the heart grew cold 'til yesterday the sun

burnt fiercely stunningly sharply straight across

my desk just before (winter) sunset

I was filled & rushed, turning off the computer

grabbing my pack & strapping it over my heavy coat

slamming open the glass door -

into darkness. The winter continues,

the money flows in month by month

little girls no more.

January 4, 2002

Woman In Training

Nancy Wallace

Frank Sinatra
Dean Martin
Dizzie Gillespie
Sammy Davis Jr.
my first mothers
from their laps
I learned the sharp glass
        of gendered landscape/ubiquitous winter
  promising summer
Their songs came into my first kitchen
as the first wife
of my first husband
Their lips made cookies
and dressed my hips
torn open by my first child
in red and yellow silks
their songs propelled me to the door
with a kiss on my mouth

first wiping the cleaned floor
& tucking the depression
into the cupboard under the sink
as my husband's steps pressed the porch
at 5 o'clock

I went to meet him at the door
so he wouldn't leave me
for the companionship of men
who understood all too well
the breakdown
of women's bodies even at nineteen
upon saying vows at the altar

my son the last to come
through my loins
prints songs he heard in the womb
onto a CD especially for me
        Frank Sinatra
        Dean Martin
        Dizzie Gillespie
and plays Elvis
in the few minutes left
before the drive to the airport
& I am unaccountably wildly
anxious.

Joe Tetro is a poet who lived in Stockton, California but has since packed up his life and moved to Mexico. He has been a regular at the Barnes & Noble and the Caffine Den readings in Stockton and the Jewel of the Valley poetry show in Lodi.

God on a Tractor

Joe Tetro

The whirling machinery's
high-pitched howling sang
in chorus with the tractor's
fuel-fired, barking staccato
from which flowed a long, swishing
river of belt powering
the whirling metal knives
of the grinder—
shredding corn
and cobs so fine
they flew like dust
up the airshaft,
down the spout,
and into a wagon . . .
a deafening, pandemonium—
like a clamoring ascension
of the iron-bound chains of hell.
Ears ringing,
with a full bucket of corn
for the chickens
loaded in my play wagon,
and my five year old sister
placed behind it,
I grab the wagon's little tin handle
and start past
the conveyor belt's
unshielded end
of hinged
and slotted steel
feeding the beast.
I glance back . . . the conveyor's
lifting my sister
by a trapped finger—

inching her like fodder—
towards the spinning blur
of knives;
I'm instantly screaming,
leaping, and waving my arms
at God on the tractor;
seeing me,
he moves like a cat,
and the howling world
of whirling knives creaks . . .
screeches . . . shudders,
and dies.
Like a divine breath
from the core of a dream—
the silence was awesome . . .
and while her pinched
and swollen finger
slipped free, my terrified heart—
still locked in my throat—
continued its wild,
uncontrollable sobbing,
and gasping for breath,
as if it were drowning—
unable to work
itself loose
from the view of the world
I'd just seen
without my sister in it.

Shawn Walker is a young poet who's traveled around the United States and writes from the heart of America. His work reflects a GenX flavor. He is an example of a young beat poet, still hungry.

Today I'm Bored

Shawn Walker

Today I'm bored.
I have no need for
instant coffee,
drive through
or even a BLAZING
LIGHTING FAST
DSL.
Today I just wanna
sit on the couch
all day long.
Watching TNT
Straight to video
Men Who Like Movies
T.V.
'Cause today
I'm gonna be just what
society and mommie said
I was
LAZY,
UNMOTIVATED
Generation X!
Yep that's me,
no time for tree hugging
Planet saving
Or now fat
used to be skinny,
"All In The Family"
Sally Struthers.
But maybe
just once every 2 hours
I'll get up
and brush off
the potato chip
crumbs.

Christina Hayes is an intriguing poet from the Sierra Nevada foothills. Her work and poetry rise out of a beautiful and creative spirit. She lives with her children, her dogs and her dreams. Her work is featured in the book, *Whispers Along The Delta* and many other venues.

Cutting Her Hair

Christina Hayes

It was like this:
we were sitting across
from each other in
booth 11 of the Somerset Diner
in Somerset, New Jersey.

My sister and I.

She was 29, and I was already
telling people I was 33
with six months left to go.

We had been talking about me taking her daughter—
Autistic,

Almost four,
Said "juice" and "kitty."

Not Mommy.
Not her name.

Of course, she couldn't leave the child with her father.
Everyone agreed.

Even *he* agreed, eventually.

She just said that perhaps the best thing
would be to place her in a good foster home
while she spent a year or so trying to get better—

To get the chemo or the surgery or whatever was necessary.

She didn't think I could do it, what with my four kids,
my job, my writing.

I leave my children, book a flight—San Francisco to Newark.

I am going to take her daughter.

She stares into her coffee cup, says,
"I trust you, you know. Because you *raised* me."

I've heard this before. I know what she's going to say next:

"Remember that day, Chris, when I came home from school, talking like the girls in my classes—I was in all those remedial classes."

"You were dyslexic—they didn't know it—"

"I know, I know, but anyway . . . "
She takes a sip of her coffee.

She remembers it like it was yesterday:
The way she adopted street slang,
a new language that popped on her tongue—
words for working out red anger,
for flare-ups and flashing—
that kind of cornered fighting
that suppresses the deep pain
of abandoned young.

The girl who had been
my fourteen-year-old sister
brought this language home—

Used it in the living room and at the table,
challenging me, defying my will
to see her raised well even in the
absence of our mother.

And I slapped her **hard** across the face with my right hand.

Fifteen years later
her hand rises to her cheek,
flushed with remembering,
then drops slowly.

I say that I still feel bad about that.

"No, you shouldn't feel bad," she leans across the table—
She's been wanting to tell me this for years:

"Remember, you said,
'Don't *ever* walk into this house again, talking trash.
The filth in your mouth is the mark of what's in your head.
It steers you—one way or another.
You decide your life every day
as simply as you choose the words you say."

I nod, remembering how I told her
I would see to it that she would do better than *that*,
better than her friend Dorothy,
fifteen with two babies already,
sharing a bedroom with her brothers
while her mother worked three jobs.

The waitress pours more coffee. We tear open plastic creamers,
turn them over into our cups.

My twenty-nine-year old sister looks at me, says
"I *did* do better than *that*.
I went to college."

I am going to take her daughter to California with me.

I am going to take her daughter.

She tells me that
it's okay with her
if her daughter calls me Mommy—

sometime in the future
when she learns to talk.

Suddenly, I feel angry, or at least I think it's anger
because it flares up like that around my ears.

And I tell her to listen to me:
That her daughter will *never* call me Mommy,
that she will learn who her mother is,
and I will be her Auntie
who loves her almost as much
as her mother did. Does.

The waitress drops the check on the table without stopping.
My sister asks if I will do
one more thing for her
before I leave.
I am going to take her daughter.
"Cut my hair."

I look at her:
the purple hollows beneath her eyes,
the cracked lips,
the tiny gold earrings in the center of the lobes.

And I look at her hair,
falling like amber,
like honey poured behind her shoulders
to the small of her back
Her hair,
splashing light back,
even the harsh light hanging
above our heads,
even that fractured light ripples and liquefies
and bounces back, warmed,
into the cool room.
Her hair
perhaps the one thing about her that her
husband still loves—

She is waiting for me to say *Yes*
because nothing else is as hard
as the way the hair falls out in the shower,
swims and swirls on the tile floor and clogs the drain,
the way it loosens in the night on the white pillow,
collects against the baseboards until you find it while
sweeping.

She thinks that maybe this time it will be
easier if she cuts it first—

She is asking me because she cannot bear to do it herself.

She is asking me to do this thing before
I leave with her daughter.

I look into my coffee—into my hands—into my lap.
I cannot look at her.

She begins to weep.

I look at her hands on the table.
"I can take your little girl," I tell her,

"for a year . . . or forever."

We both know that it may come to that.
We have already said this to each other.
"I'll quit my job,

stop writing—whatever it takes,
to carry her for you.
I will pick out flowers

and give her your amethyst ring—
if it comes to that, you know I will."

We can hear each other breathing.
"But I cannot cut your hair,"

I tell her. Just like that.

She goes to the bathroom.

I put three dollars on the table, get up,
and walk to the glass doors.

I am going to take her daughter.

In the morning,

she stands at her kitchen sink—
all that long hair gone.

Rebecca Morrison is the founder of the Third Sunday Writers Group of Sacramento, California. She was born in Arizona and raised in a small Russian fishing village in Alaska. Ms. Morrison is a UC Davis graduate. Her poetry can be found on the web at www.eskimopie.net

Rapture (while kayaking on Lake Natomas)

Rebecca Morrison

Like a bird of prey
I fall headlong
from turquoise sky
into tar-black water
diving for a
subsurfaced glint
a cool bass
flashing back and forth
in ecstatic
wag of water
on water
I sun surface
glide my keel
slice, I cut
out huge mouthfuls
of dark sparklings
like a gray raptor
child of air
I tear into wetness
with body
and tongue I devour
blue
leaning sharply
leaving a
blue plume
serpentine-like
I weave wind
into my sail of
light
I rip/slash paddle
displace that
underness
which bears me
like strong arms
pushing
water knocks
I answer
raptor
I met on the
open morning
she cries sharp
my beak
opens
blue blood running
from my mouth

Curtis Fletcher is a dot.com poet, who lives in Colorado, works in California and writes across the friendly skies of hope. He is a poet, writer, actor, football player, dramatist, improv performer, singer and spiritual leader. He is a force behind DCW for business.

For Godspell

Curtis Fletcher

From different places
we come to the dance
bound to each other
beyond circumstance
and though I may see
only what you allow
a piece of my heart
belongs to you now
so come let us dance
let enchantment begin
let fly the wind magic
you carry within
and together we'll be
more than each of us seems
the makers of music
and dreamers of dreams

Marie Ross began writing poetry following the death of her husband to console herself. Her works have been read in many places since then and her poems console far beyond herself. She is a Stockton, California resident.

"The Day The Eagle Cried"

Marie Ross

The eagle cried that darkened day
as two planes so swiftly sped,

And crashed two mighty buildings
that left all too many dead.

He reached out from his feathers
to cup those desperate cries,

And tried to fluff reality from the
waters of their eyes.

He scraped the ash of cinders from
his talons touching down,

As he wept and swept his heartbeats
over the hurt upon the ground.

And the winds surrounded so his
mighty wings might sour.

The tear he shed that dreadful day
he will shed forevermore.

May his strength and magnificence
always fly free in the skies over
our great nation.

“Oh Honored Stone”

Marie Ross

We stand here now to touch this stone

placed in memory,

Of those who fought and those who died

to shape our history.

We clear our mind and quickly find the honor

they bestowed,

From land and sea and silver planes so freedom

we could hold.

This stone captures life and death from the

silence of its sound.

And from the patriotic breezes of souls, lifting up

to sacred ground.

This poem is engraved in granite
at the Lodi, California All Veteran’s Plaza

Bob Bartholomew has long had his poetry used by his church in bulletins, newsletters, etc. In 2002 he produced his first book, *Seed,* which is a collection of a lifetime's work. He is retied and lives with his wife, Esther, in Lodi, California.

Green Grass

Bob Bartholomew

Desert sun, rough grit, baked earth, rocks bare
        of life;
each object a symbol of hardship and strife.

Yet this parched soil and gritty sand,
        unyielding rocks bare God's own hand.

For these same cruel rocks give shade to few,
        at times they catch the morning dew.

And on the north you may see
        some form of life and more to be.

Could be in time, only our God knows;
        it may be where the green grass grows.

Virgil Dughi was born, raised and educated in the San Joaquin Valley, and except for a tour with the Army and a short mistake of a move to LaLa Land, he's lived here his whole life. He says, "I think I am beginning to enjoy it." Virgil is a regular reader at Barnes & Noble in Modesto, California.

Improvisation

Virgil Dughi

I wanna write
poetry spontaneously
improvisational poems
that spring from
an inner simplicity
lost in revision
lost in thought

I wanna rebop
into bebop
play words like
notes on Miles'
trumpet
on Adderly's
sax
on Bill Evens'
ivory keys

I want my pages
to play smooth
subtle jazz
that vibrates
in the mind
of my reader

Stephanie Freeman is the mother of three and a physics student. She has published two chapbooks, *Burning, Burning, All is Burning* and *Evolution of a Woman.* She has read on radio, televison and at various venues in the Bay Area and Central Valley.

(Untitled) Stephanie Freeman

I watch as my house
burns to the ground
wondering how long
before it cools enough
for me to dance in ashes.

I will mix ashes
with rainwater
streak my face and my hair
perform a war dance
defying the struggles
of my unforeseeable fate.

I will roll in the ashes
emerging like a Jewish mother
carrying her firstborn out of Egypt
through the howls and screams
of Egyptian mothers cradling their dead.

Ashen ghost dancer, I will dance
with the crazy hope and pain
that died with this house.
I live ghost in the past,
warrior in the future,
presently, impatiently
watching my house
burn to the ground.

Poet, painter, and spatial kinetic artist, **John Thomas Mead** is co-founder, along with Frank Andrick, of AMP Press. He has co-produced poetry programs at Sonora's Stage Three Theater, Luna's Café, the Sacramento Poetry Center, the Michael Himovitz Gallery as well as many other Northern California locations. He has produced the compilation CD Three Poets Tour and his own CD of poetic soundings called Un-metered Calculus. His book of poems Selenium includes his own illustrations and a preface by San Francisco poet/professor Neeli Cherkovski.

An Untutored Memo to Robinson Jeffers

John Thomas Mead

"You are all dead! Dead I say!"
No, not even the servant's blanket under the aged oak
could ease the cold and feign the light
All the wild flowers on the fallen hills
could not answer, not a word, not a single word
Even the Cyprus has died and the ink has faded into a
different season

The Spanish animal trainer may have left a throne
But remember that the animals only dance when tricked,
they are not civilized
And the river rages against the wall
And the flesh is eaten one piece at a time
the desert flowers bloom and die before they reach your muse
do not dissolve into an alcoholic bliss
because hell is a difficult vision and it has
killed art far too often
Even a circling hawk now only roams in the depths of dark
cities

I do not expect love, you are correct
"expectations bring great sorrows
and no soul deserves the more troubled energies"

but have I experienced it?
I have seen god there, once
dreams are true, you are correct
I am frightened,
I frighten

Maybe it is only one language
Maybe it is the ancient homeland
Maybe it is violence, have you killed lately?
Maybe it is consumption of the singularity
Maybe it is a small instruction on numbers
Maybe it is a large sanctuary with no word of God
Maybe it is the low levels
one wonders

In the histories of lost stallions
the tongues are tied to dying trees

Love Song For The Shrike

John Thomas Mead

I saw your love tokens
nailed upon the picket fence
for me or the next
it made no difference
as each offering was a song
played upon the deep throated pike
and all the little creatures
the amoric display of the shrike

Late Night Vigilance

John Thomas Mead

They are all up late tonight
tonight

in small metal buildings
up late, again, like every night
up late with the stars and the dogs
up late, waiting for the cold morning

They are sitting alone with the night before day
and yesterday
huddled around oak, or small fire
with the lonely lights and memorabilia
They are sitting alone again
with heads bowed and eyes lowered,
with hands in pockets
They are sitting up late tonight
with tasks and assignments
yielded to them with hurried hands
like lost notes and folded papers
They are up late tonight in heavy coats
wrapped tight around them
with them, alone
in the darkness

ready for the luminary and the sudden
that which is on the edge, waiting
steady to the reason in midnight vision
dreamt by them in the small rooms
and behind stairs
coddled and cold, carefully attended, carefully
for each his own regularity
its singular and the heartbeat
for each a secure return to rise and element
a final nod for they are . . .

up late again
for us
tonight

Brian Lawrie lives in Aberdeen, Scotland near the Highlands, "climbed and walked there all my days." He is a member of a group of poets centered around Storm Magazine. Every anthology should have a ghost poet, ours is from Scotland.

Jewels for Dewa

Brian Lawrie

Two days
since the great rains
and you've relented

Half drowned
riverside companions
breathe again

All
along the bank,
iridescent
in the grasses,
on the twigs of the cherry,
on withered bramble,
along the willow branches,
high on the towering beeches,
(even the dead bracken
has an offering)

A magnificent
reconciliation
is condensing in the air,
defying gravity;
string upon string
of glimmering pearls,
perfectly round

Jewels for Dewa

her torment over

Luke Breit is the author of five books of poetry, *Unintended Lessons*, his latest joins, *Celebrating America Within, Words the Air Speaks, In This Picture, We Are Laughing* and *Messages: New & Selected Poems*. He is the President of the Sacramento Poetry Center.

The Right Way
Luke Breit
For John Fremont

Dear John,
There is no one way to do anything.
You know that, I know that,
no matter the number of times
you go back to the drawing board
thinking this time you'll get it right.
It could be the woman, the drink,
the dinner, the weekend with the kids,
the job, the poem, the novel,
the way you comport yourself under stress.
They can't even figure out if there's
one right way to get into heaven,
or what it is, harps on billowy clouds
or the guiltless brothel we've always hoped.
After all is said and done, though,
you move exponentially closer to getting it right
to the degree that the end swims into focus
and starts shutting your options down.
If there's only one or two ways to move,
how can you get it wrong? You're right
at least 50 percent of the time and,
if you're not, stay out of Reno or even
the Indian casino on the way to the coast.
I know we say there's no hell, but what if
as the tunnel opened flames licked at your heels,

man, how you'd try to hoist yourself back over the lip
of life, cling to what you know,
get one more chance to do it right,
figure out the choices you never saw.

Roger Ernesto Naylor is a long time Stockton poet who has appeared in many different poetry readings in Northern California, including "Poetry Unplugged", "Jewel of the Valley", Maxwell's Bookmark, The Poet's Corner, etc.

How He Made His Bones

Roger Ernesto Naylor

Of parchment skin and tellum bones
lying old dogs and professional gnomes
how trick green briar sleeves
soured root beer to make it bleed

Of endeary spearmints of pebbled love
so good humility bow encore to stars above
how harvest sugarcane become marzipan
this simple hired player his ergo sum

Of indeterminate inquiry and inquest
the mockery of living life and dying death
how angelic cantata gave credence to rumort
nail-bit Midas touch none more gloomier

Of dic, screwed too tight, too many marbles
song of many bosses and crosses canary warbles
how puzzling over pieces frames a bigger picture
soundless scream disease aids but no cure

Of Afric moon technicolor, crescendo shatter in ovation
not so old or blue not cycle anew in rebirth of creation
how pill tax disconcerted with lack of precipitant urge
over dark, unstinting glade late dry loon, love-lorn bird

Of sermons on mustard seeds to serpent eggs and clouds
appeal to country of Greek letters, the twins appian proud
how the hundred—eyed ibis hold sacred piscus enbeaked
hail Ich Dien, ram-horned reindeer come to feast

Of mire, mud hole, quicksand, sty, to worst compare
no crooked laxness rule, statute, law, judgement spare
how guilt reveals the guilty, stringiness the miser
no unsullied, unsoiled pardon or fealty miserly Kaiser

Of faith and love abiding in fellowship and humanity
against the demons of vain hate and power's inanity
how vile injustice and war may be brought to book
straightened brought from crooked hitch, hang-up, hook

Of love so apoplectic, of death so spasmodic
the remorseless has not yet ceased its terrible tic
how can love conquer all while death defend hideous hell
life athward, held back from power to light darkest dell

Of this tome, this toll, this pacing outside a tomb
of love of life, country, world may be so presumed
how pen laid down for consideration's sake
a gift a hope of moisture sore lips to slake

Of this now let careful listener append
these in sacred trust, these words the poet sends
how, now, a world's salvation is at stake
around campfires, people discuss destiny, human fate